Elora Ontario in Colour Photos, Saving Our History One Photo at a Time

Photography
by Barbara Raue
updated 2016

Series Name:
Cruising Ontario

Book 69: Elora

Cover photo: Reflections on the water

Series Name: Cruising Ontario
Saving Our History One Photo at a Time

Series Name: Cruising Ontario
Saving Our History One Photo at a Time

Book 120-121: Amherstburg
Book 122: Essex
Book 123-124: Kingsville
Book 125-127: Woodstock
Book 128: Thamesford
Book 129-132: St. Marys
Book 133-136: Sarnia
Book 137-138: Welland
Book 139-144: Kingston

Other Books by Barbara Raue

Coins of Gold –biography of May Todd

Arrows, Indians and Love – historical fiction

The Life and Times of Barbara
Volume 1: Inventions That Have Enhanced My Life
Volume 2: Entertainment That I Have Enjoyed
Volume 3: East Coast Trips
Volume 4: Olympics Have Always Intrigued Me
Volume 5: Wonders of the World
Volume 6: Caribbean Cruises We Have Enjoyed
Volume 7: Animals
Volume 8: Storms and Other Major Disasters in My Lifetime
Volume 9: Wars, Terrorist Attacks and Major Disasters

The Cromwell Family Book

Laura Secord Discovered – historical fiction

Daddy Where Are You? - Memoir

Visit Barbara's website to view all of her books
http://barbararaue.ca

Elora is located in Wellington County on the Grand River and is about twenty kilometers north of Guelph, and twenty kilometers northeast of Kitchener-Waterloo.

Elora was founded in 1832 by Captain William Gilkison, a British officer recently returned from India. Gilkison named the community after his brother's ship, which was itself inspired by the Elora Caves near Aurangabad, Maharashtra, India.

The Elora Gorge, located at the western edge of the village, is one of the most scenic areas in Southern Ontario with its limestone cliffs descending 80 feet into the Grand and Irvine rivers where small caves, rapids, falls and quiet waters beckon visitors.

At the foot of Mill Street stands the Elora Mill, one of the few early Ontario five-storey grist mills still in existence.

David Boyle, born in Scotland in 1842, came to Canada in 1856 and settled in this area. As a local school teacher, he began an extensive collection of native artifacts and became an archaeological authority. In 1886, Boyle was appointed the first curator of the Provincial Archaeological Museum in Toronto. He was dedicated to the study and retention of artifacts and he initiated an active programme of excavation and acquisition. Through his work on Ontario prehistory, Boyle gained international recognition as a leading Canadian archaeologist and anthropologist.

When Elora first established itself as an agricultural supply center in the mid-nineteenth century, farmers coming from the north were greeted by a wagon and carriage factory, a lumber yard, blacksmith shops, and a farm implement enterprise.

Connon's Block stood at the gateway to the village on the northeast corner of Geddes and Moir Streets. It was built by Thomas Connon in 1867, housed his photography studio upstairs and living quarters in the rear. Thomas' son John joined the business and also helped to run a small grocery store in the building. He was an avid collector of local stories and documents and wrote, *The Early Years of Elora and Vicinity*.

For most of the nineteenth century the west side of Geddes Street was known as the Fair Grounds, home to the monthly Cattle Fair and periodic Horse Fairs. Andrew Gordon opened a shop in the flat iron building which he shared with hotelier Robert Dalby. Gordon ensured that the Cattle Fairs would continue to be held near his shop by spreading salt on the ground for the cows and encouraging farmers to gather at this location.

The first Town Hall was built on the Fair Grounds in 1874 and this busy intersection became the centre of the village. The Town Hall was also referred to as the Market House where market stalls were available to vendors. It also housed the village jail. It was demolished in 1960.

The row of shops on the east side of Geddes Street took full advantage by establishing their block as the main commercial hub of Elora. Businesses on this stretch of Geddes Street included hardware and dry goods merchants, grocers, tailors, shoemakers, jewellers, blacksmiths, barbers, and a music store. The music store was built, owned and operated by William Stafford beginning in 1868. A few doors north was Alexander Kerr's butcher shop; the Kerr family remained in the meat business for one hundred and twenty years.

The Trader's Bank located near the old Market Square on the northwest corner of Geddes and Colborne Street, and the Merchant's Bank near the southern edge of the square on Metcalfe Street. The new Post Office with its impressive clock tower was erected near the Town Hall in 1911 and the square was a popular meeting place. The east side of Geddes Street continues to be a prime business strip in the village core.

The Mill at Elora

Towering 100 feet above the thundering falls of the Grand River, the Mill at Elora has stood for over 150 years as a symbol of what the combined energies of man and nature can achieve. Although attempts to harness the river's power were made as early as 1817, Elora's founder, Captain William Gilkinson, was the first to seriously plan a mill. In 1832, Gilkinson, of Irvine, Scotland, purchased 14,000 acres of land around the falls for a reported $2.50 an acre. Recently retired from the Lake service with the Northwest Fur Trading Company, the Captain wrote often of his dreams of building a fine community including a Mill. In reply to one such letter, his brother noted similarity of the caves near the falls to the famous Elora Temple of India - the community now had a name. Unfortunately, Gilkinson's dreams died with him the following year. Ten years later when Elora had become a settlement of twenty-five families, Ross and Company purchased the two acres of land on which the Mill currently exists and commissioned a local carpenter (a future miller), Charles Allan. He eventually bought out the powered four runs of stone for grinding oats and barley. With the Mill in operation, the Village grew dramatically reaching a population of 1200 by the late 1850s.

In July 1859, fire demolished all but a few outbuildings. A team of thirty Scottish masons, hired by the new owner, J.M. Fraser, worked feverishly for $0.75 a day to rebuild the Mill. Using stone quarried along the river banks, a new structure was completed by the end of the year. The base of the west wall (towards the stable) was at least five feet thick and rose eight stories (over 100 feet) above the Gorge. Fire ravaged the Mill again in 1870 and again it was rebuilt, this time largely within the stone façade that survives to this day.

Today one of the most poignant reminders of the Mill's heritage is the two millstones which now rest near the entrance to the property. Each run stone consisted of a stationary lower stone (bedstone) and an upper revolving stone (the runner). Four feet wide and a foot thick, they weigh up to a ton and turned as many as one hundred and fifty revolutions per minute.

Like a torch, The Tooth of Time, long known as the Islet Rock, is perched in the middle of the falls at the beginning of four miles of a water-carved limestone ravine extending from the foot of the Mill.

The last miller to operate the property came to the district in 1928. Norman Drimmie purchased the Mill in 1944 and operated it as a custom feed and Lumber Mill until 1974 when it was sold to be renovated into its present form as Elora Mill Inn, Restaurant and Spa.

Table of Contents

Elora

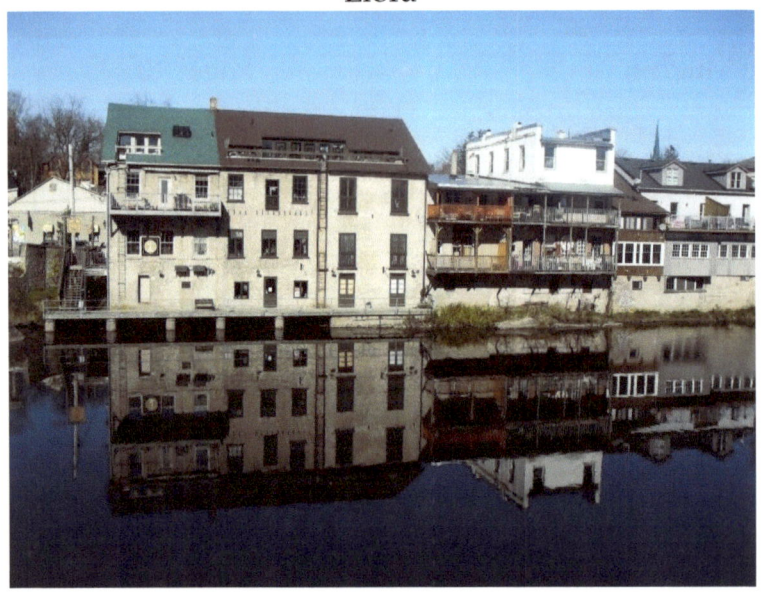

Reflections

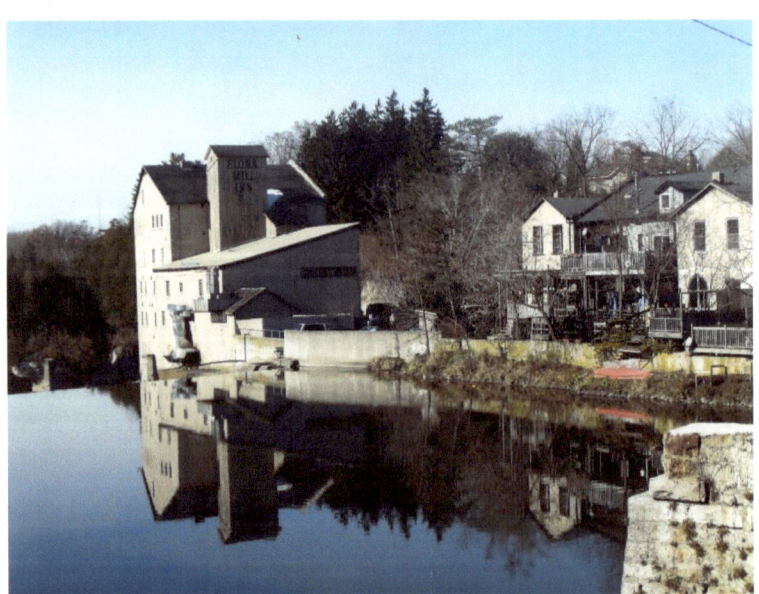

The Old Mill Inn

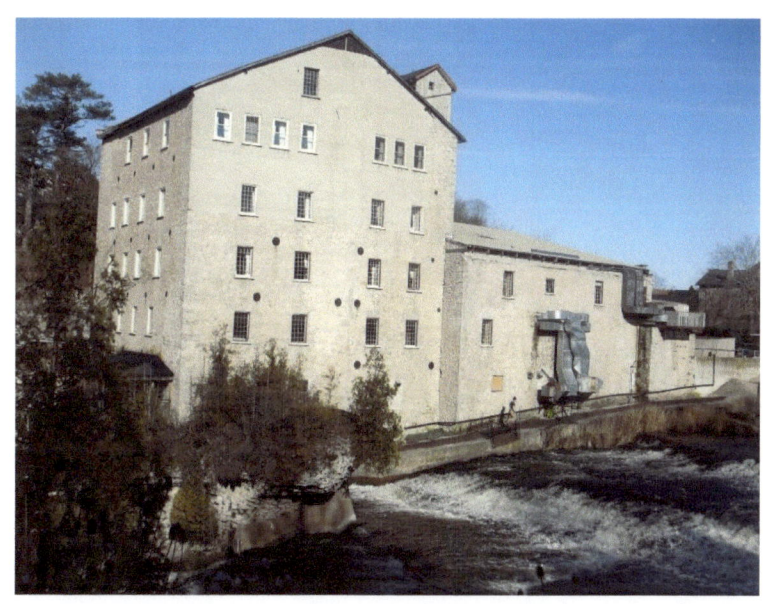

Elora Mill Inn

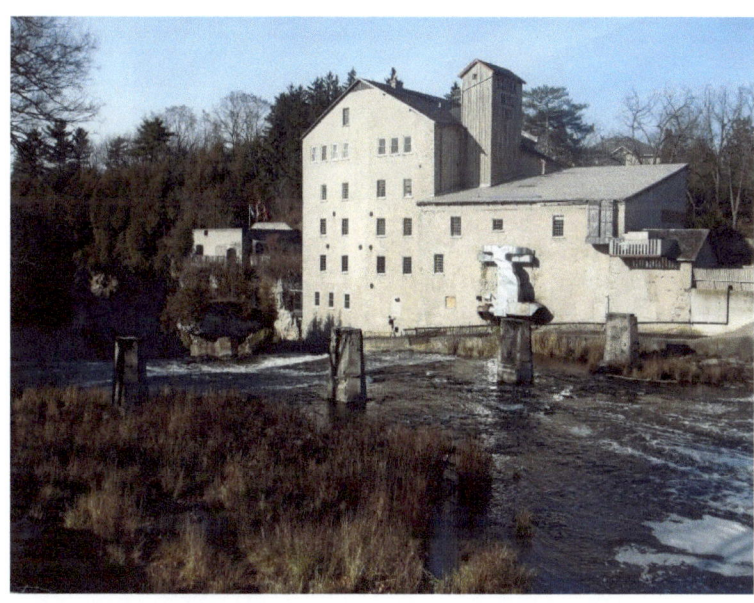

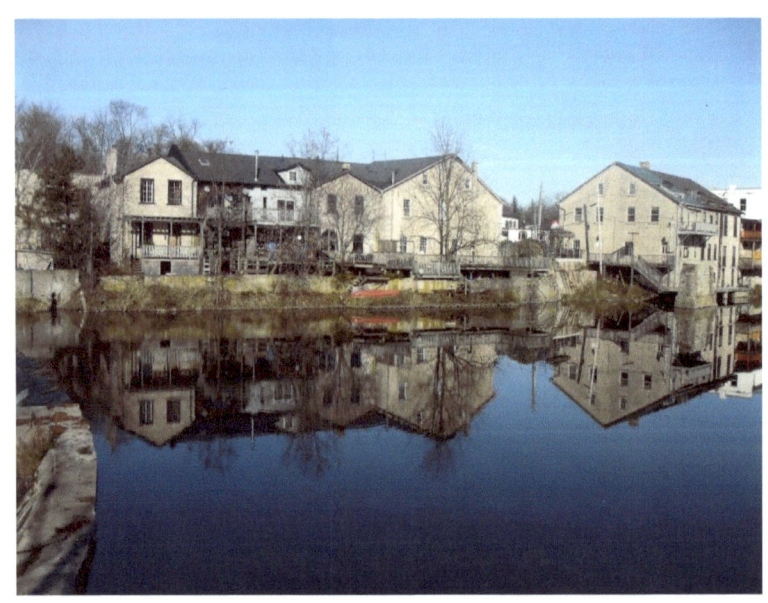

Reflections

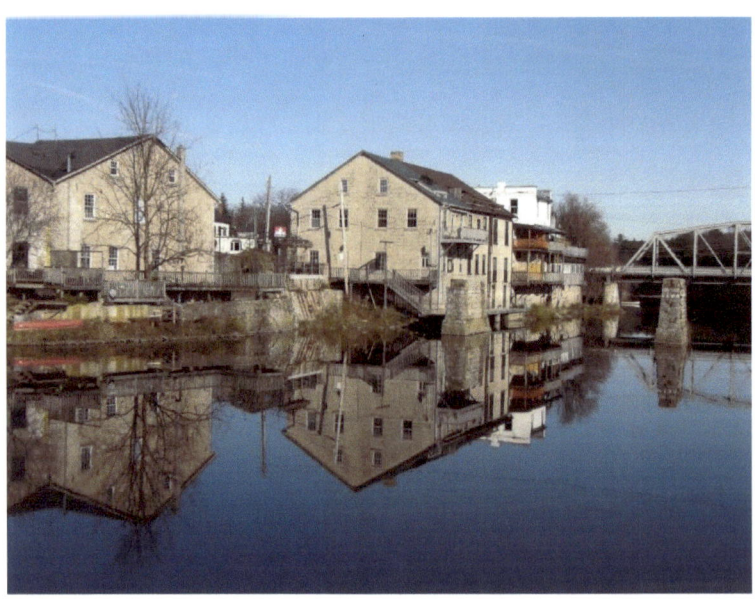

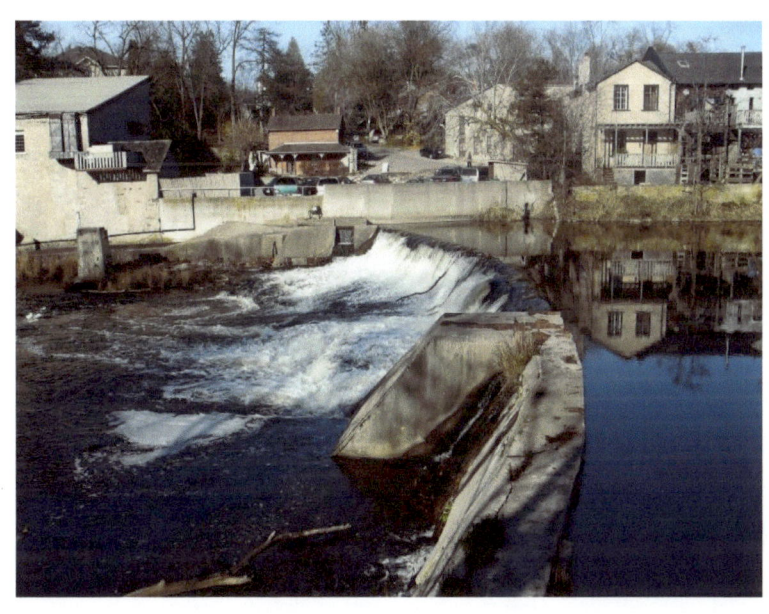

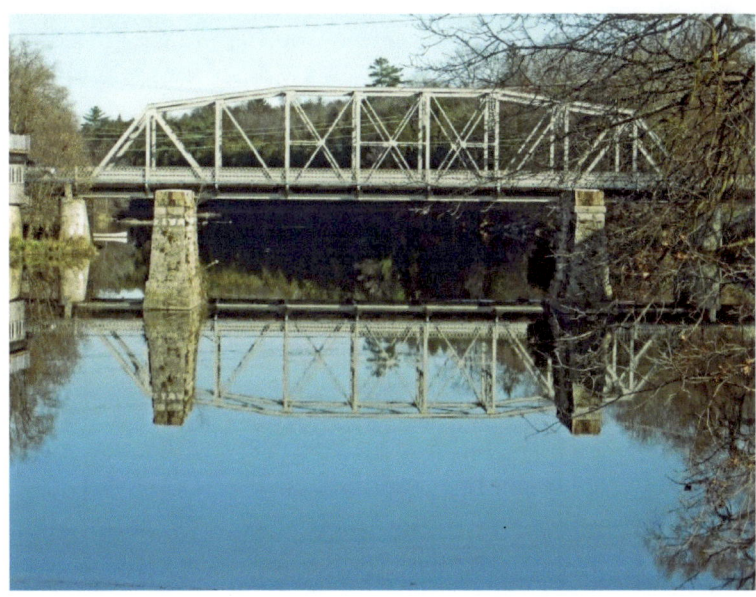

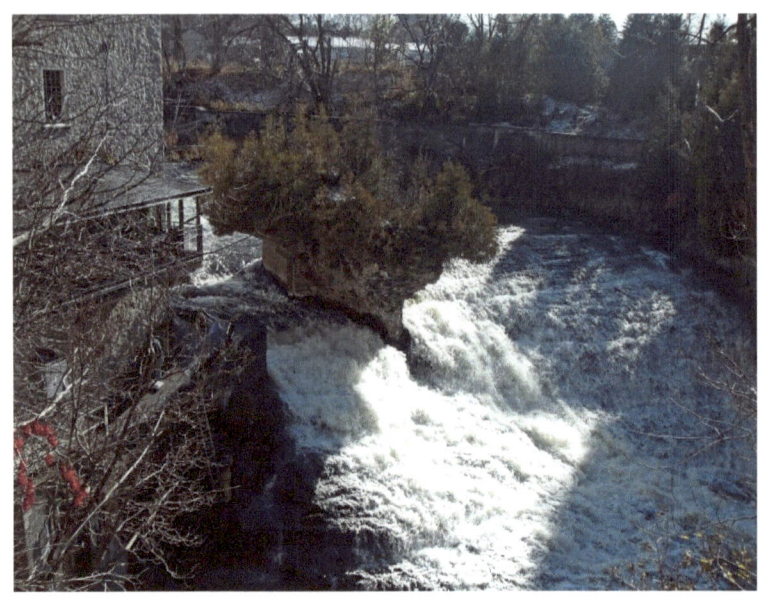

The power of water

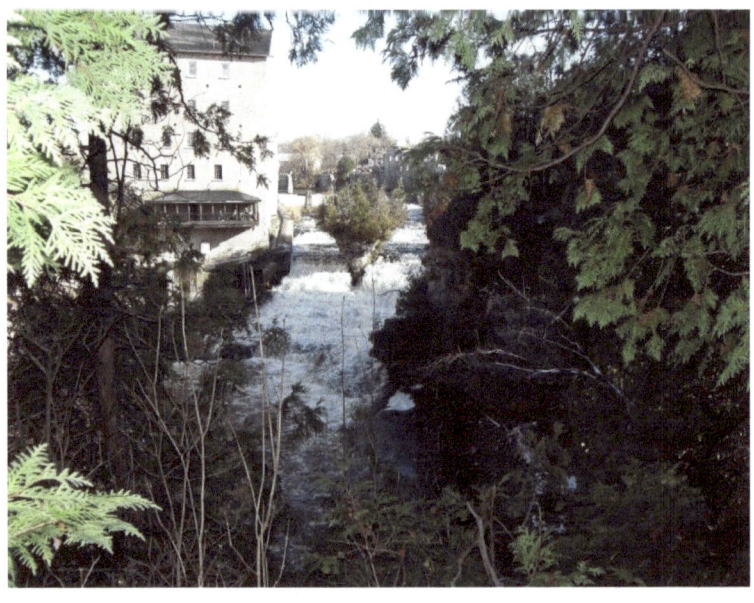

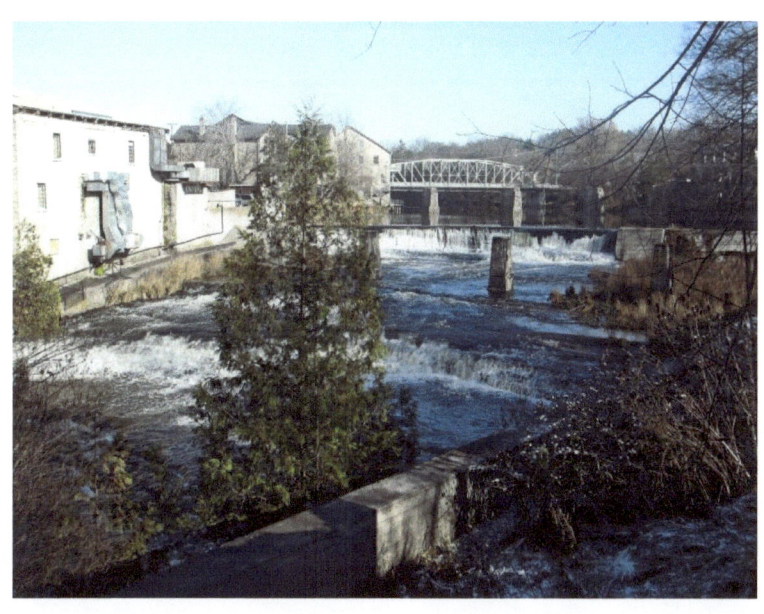

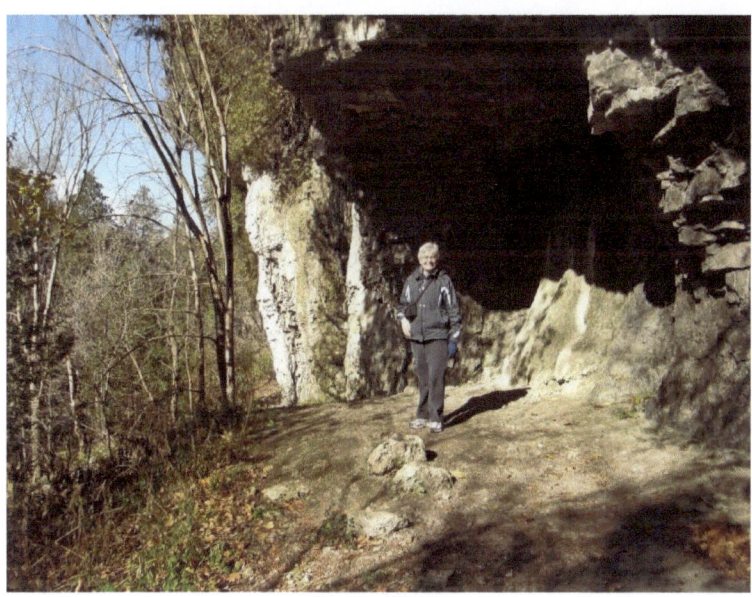

Elora Gorge

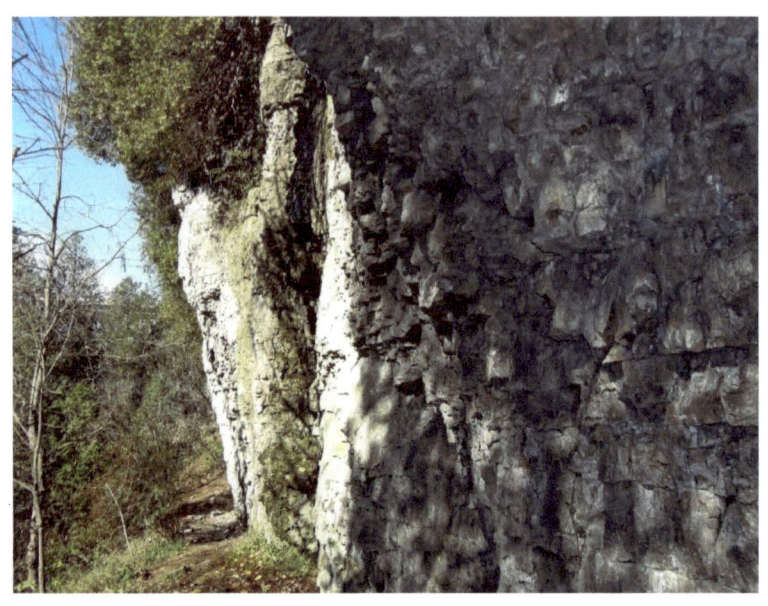

Elora Gorge

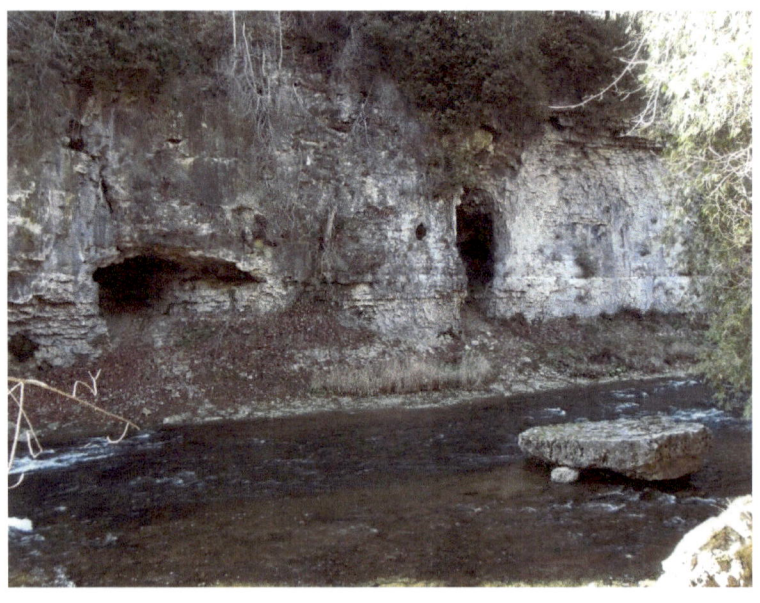

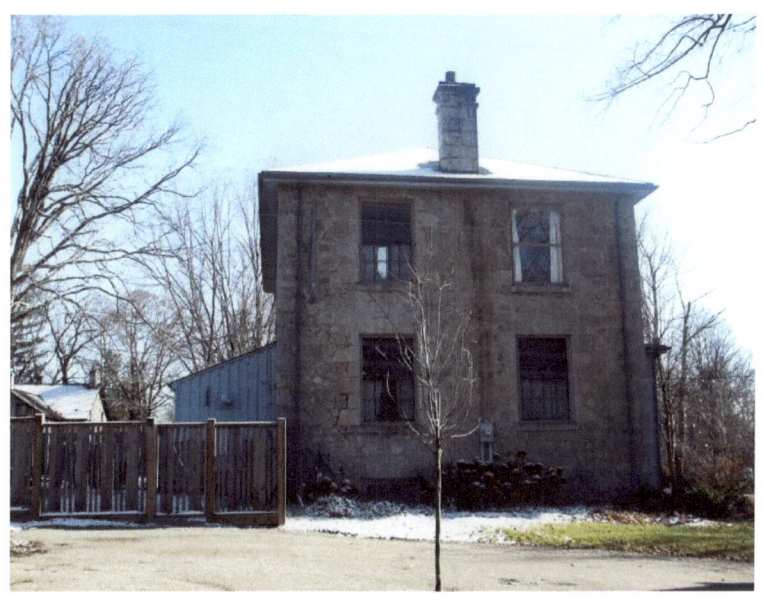

Old stone building – Italianate style

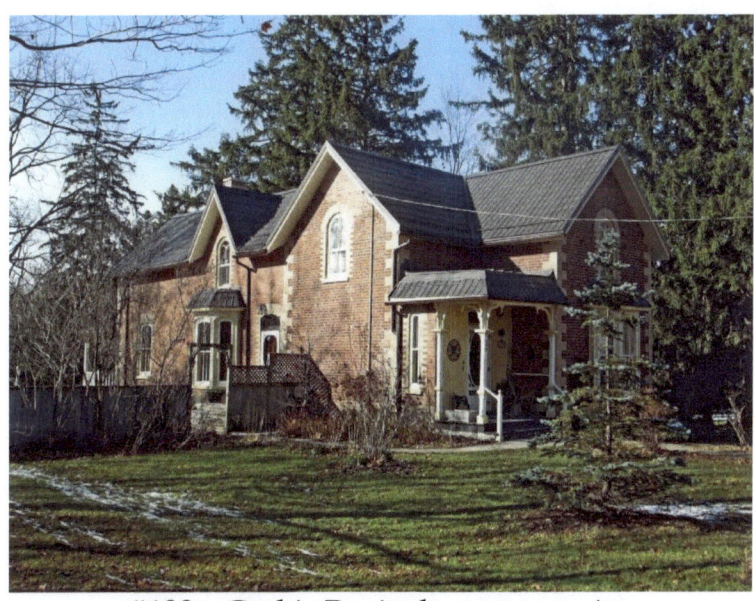

#190 – Gothic Revival, corner quoins

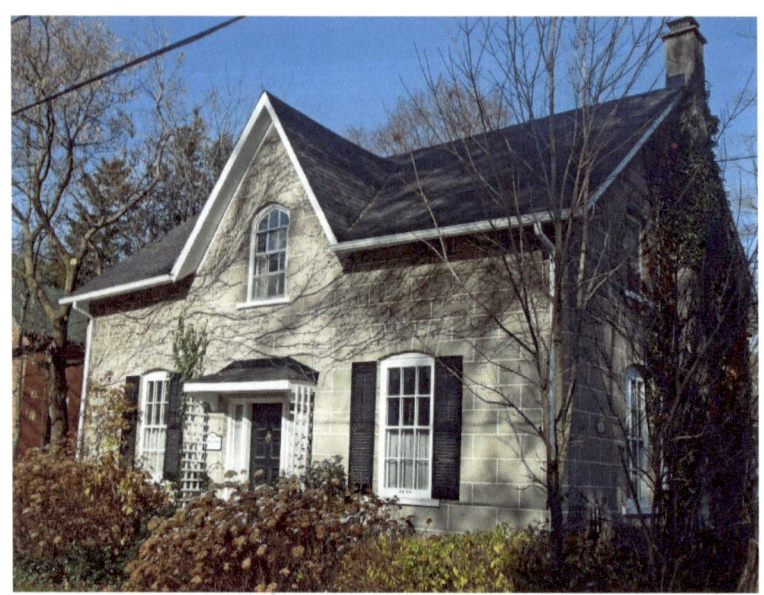

The Misses Gilbert School for Young Ladies – c. 1870
Gothic Revival cottage

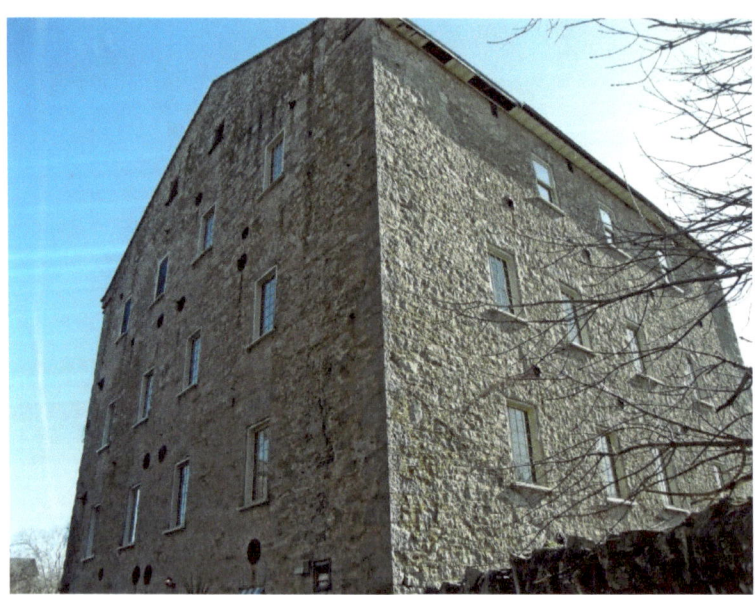

Limestone

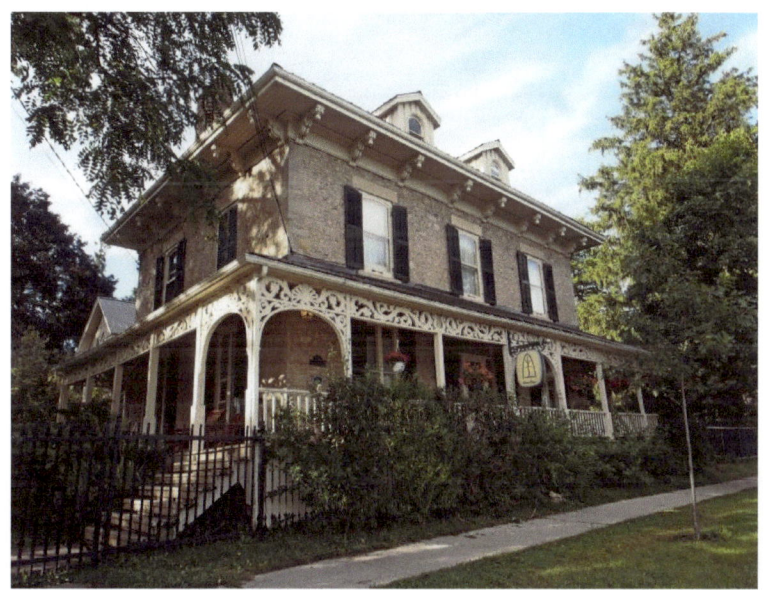

120 Mill Street East – Drew House - Italianate style – dormers in attic, single cornice brackets, wraparound verandah with bric-a-brac

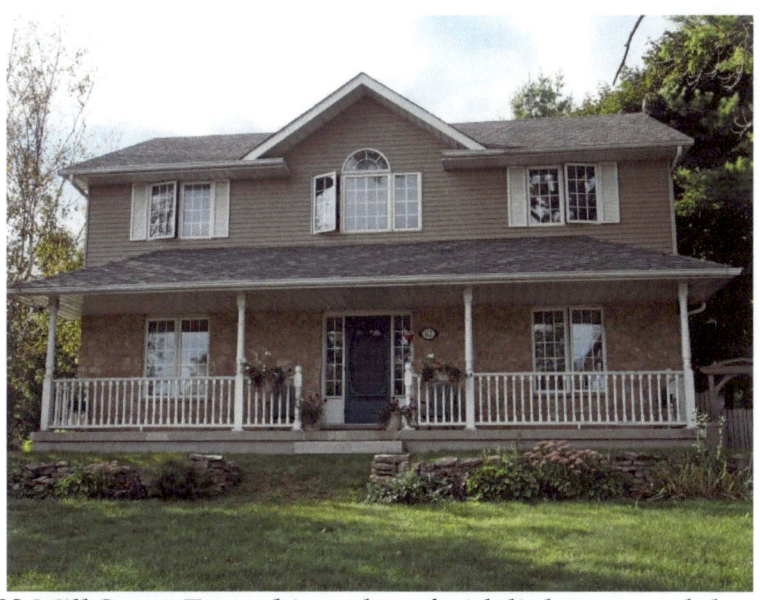

82 Mill Street East – hipped roof, sidelights around door

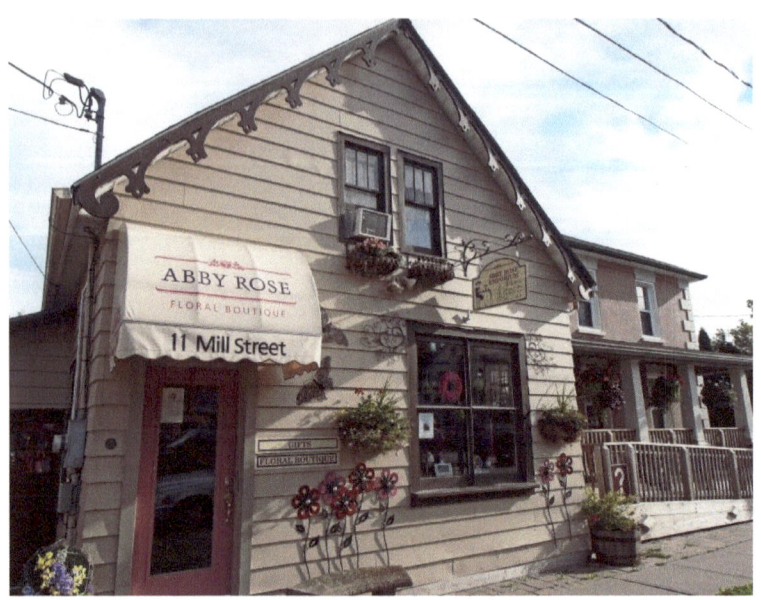

11 Mill Street East – Gothic Revival, verge board trim on gable

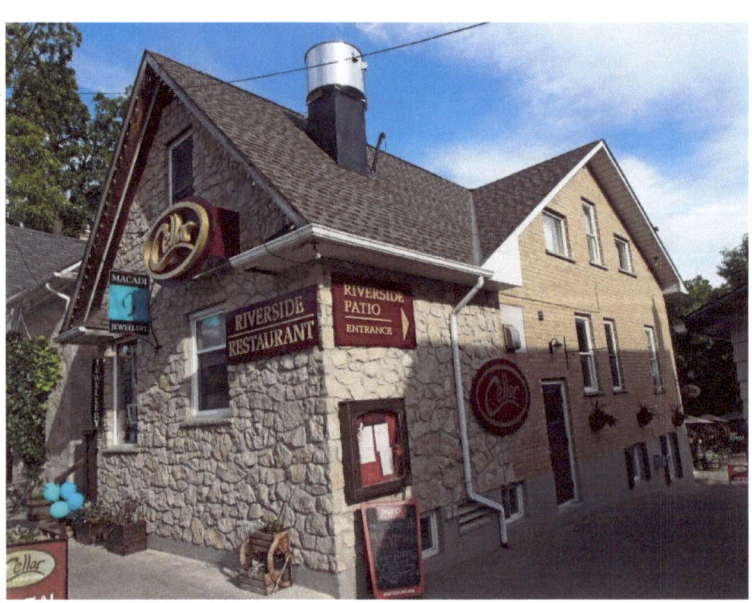

Mill Street East – limestone, cornice return on end gable

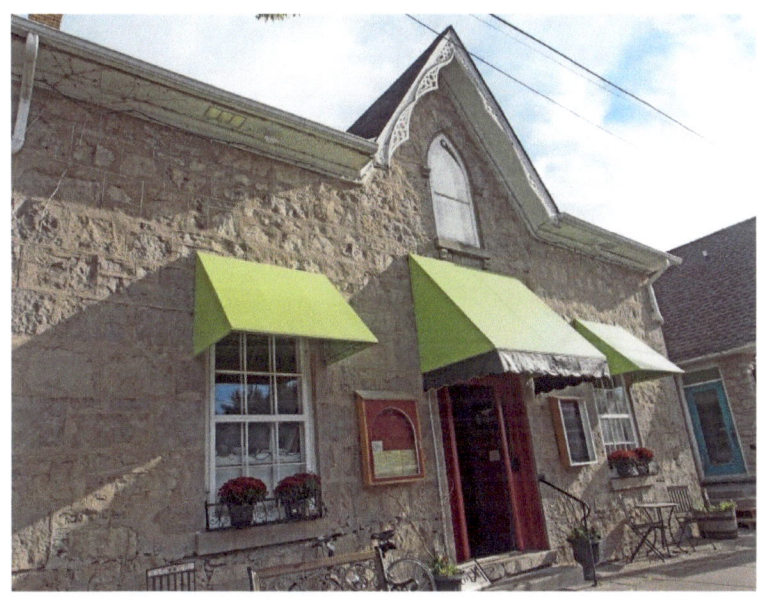

Mill Street East – Gothic Revival, limestone, verge board trim
on gable, cornice return on end gable

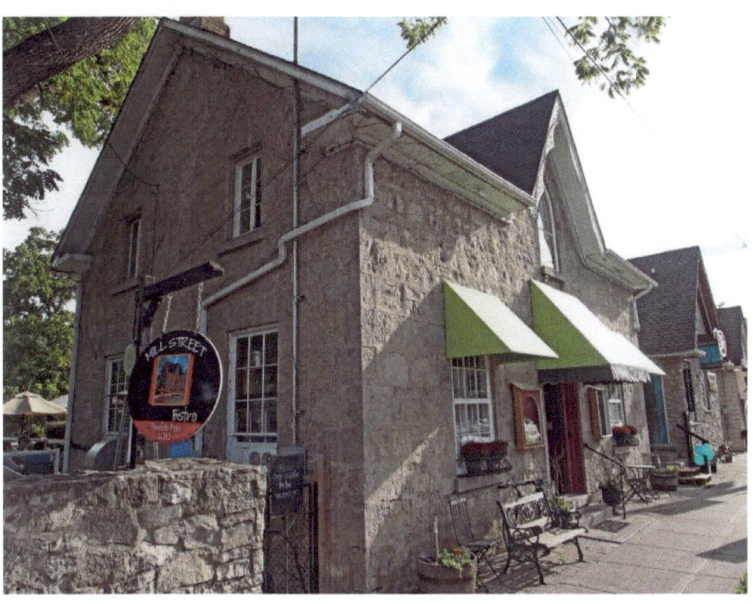

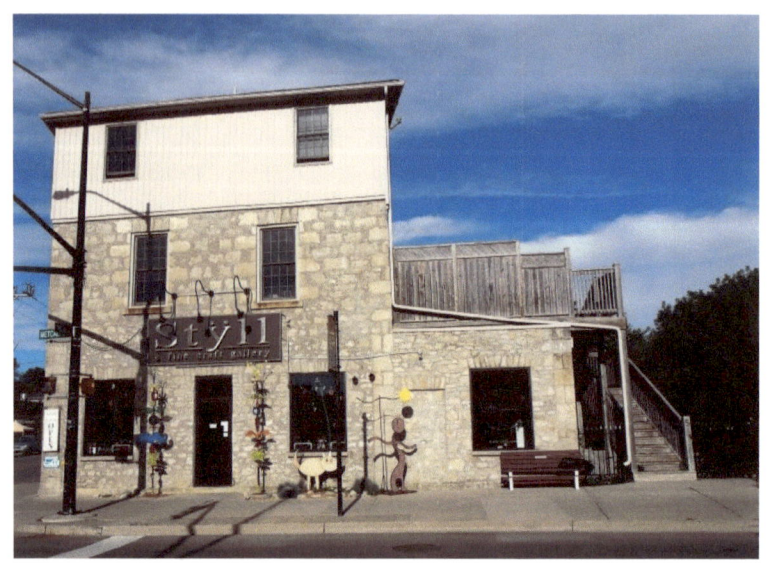

Corner of Mill and Metcalfe Streets - limestone

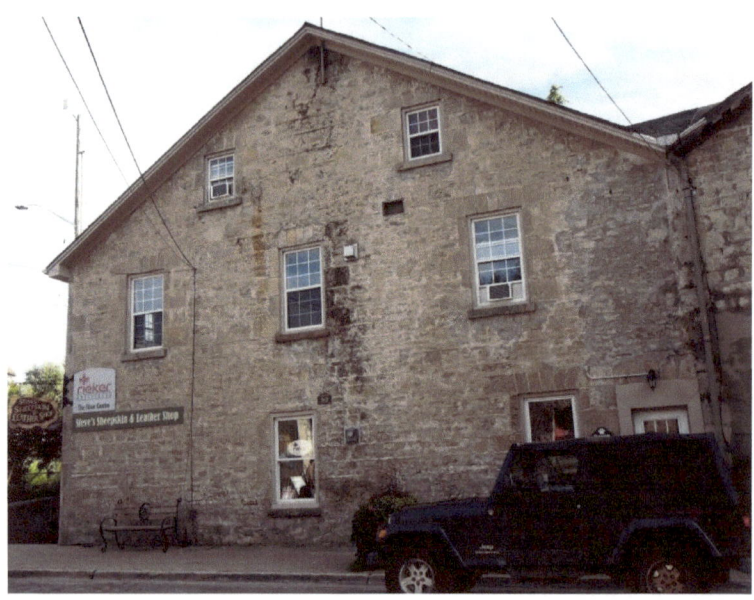

Mill Street East - limestone

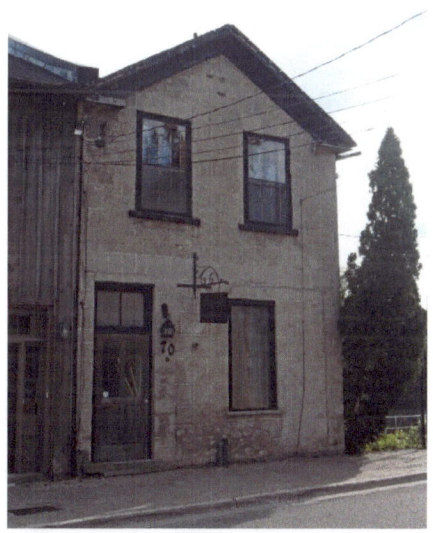

70 Mill Street East – Elora Mill Inn - limestone

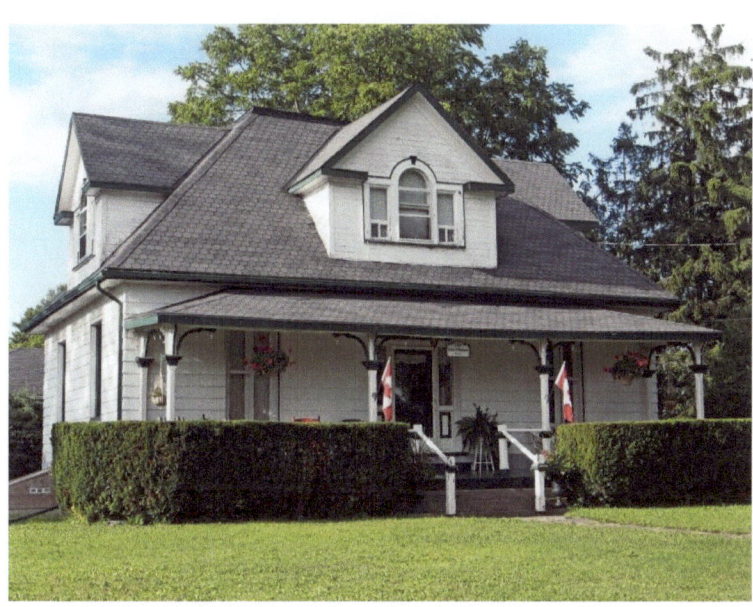

Church Street – Walter P. Newman, Banker c. 1854 – dormers
in steeply pitched hip roof, Palladian window in dormer

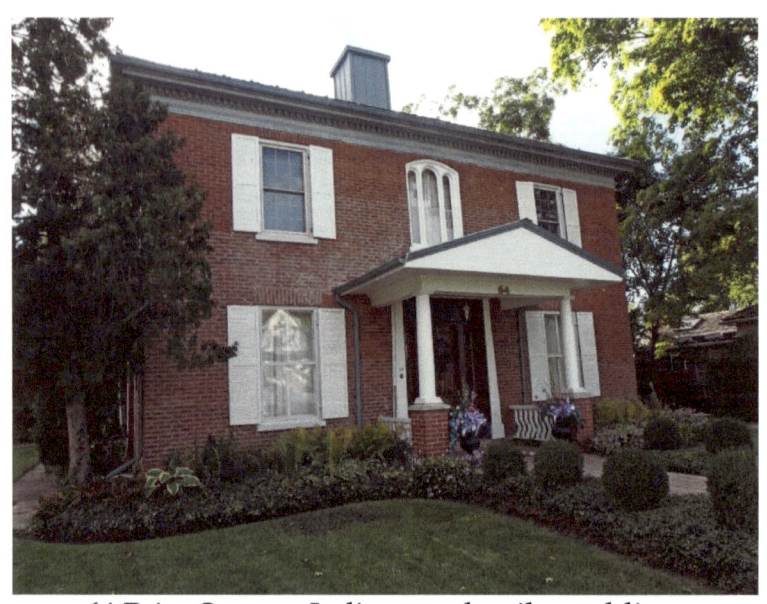

64 Price Street – Italianate, dentil moulding,
pediment above porch

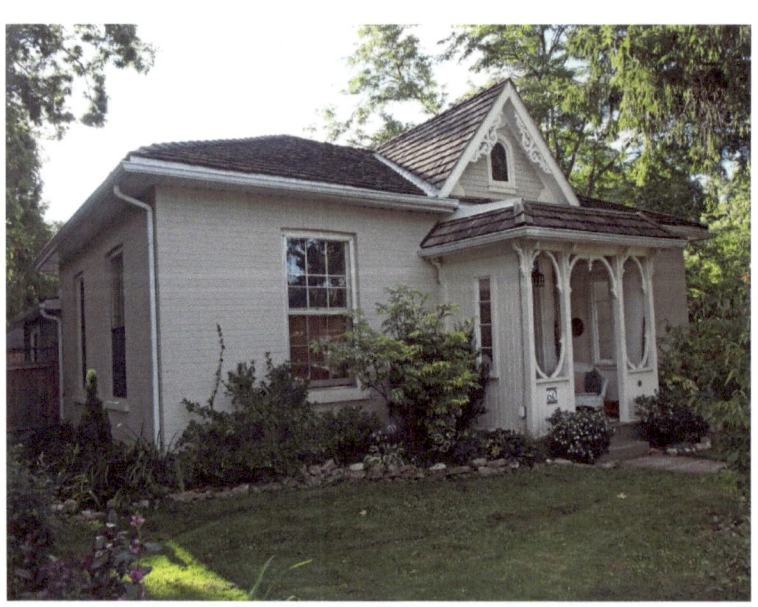

60 Price Street – Gothic Revival – verge board trim on gable,
bric-a-brac on porch

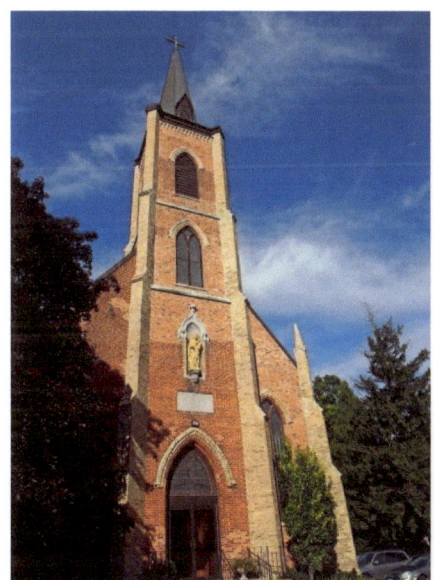
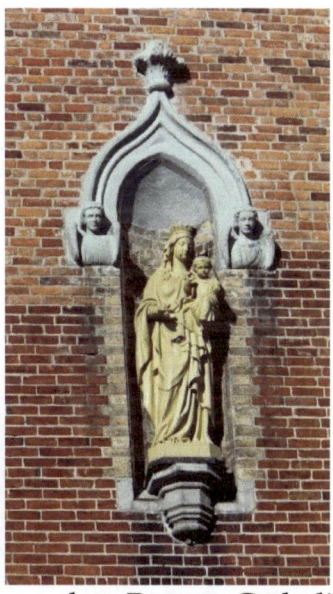

267 Geddes Street – St. Mary Immaculate Roman Catholic Church – built in 1870-71 – Gothic Revival, buttresses, lancet windows

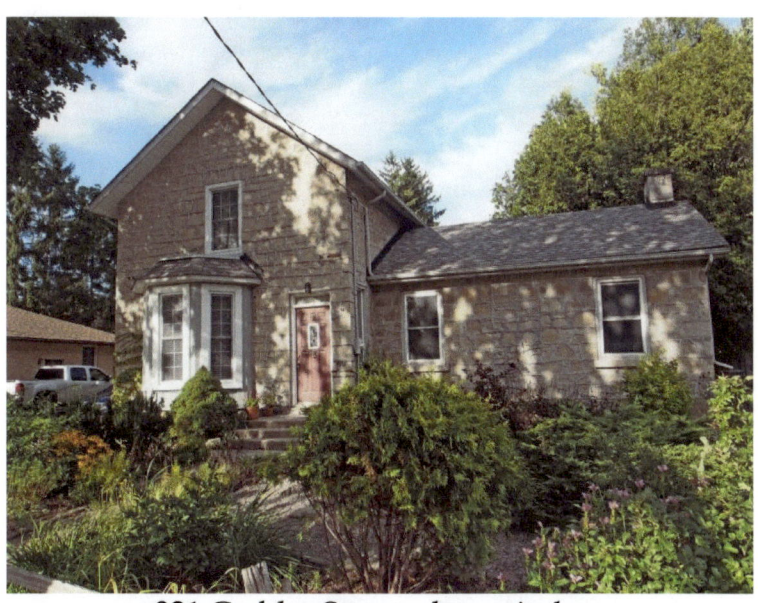

321 Geddes Street – bay window

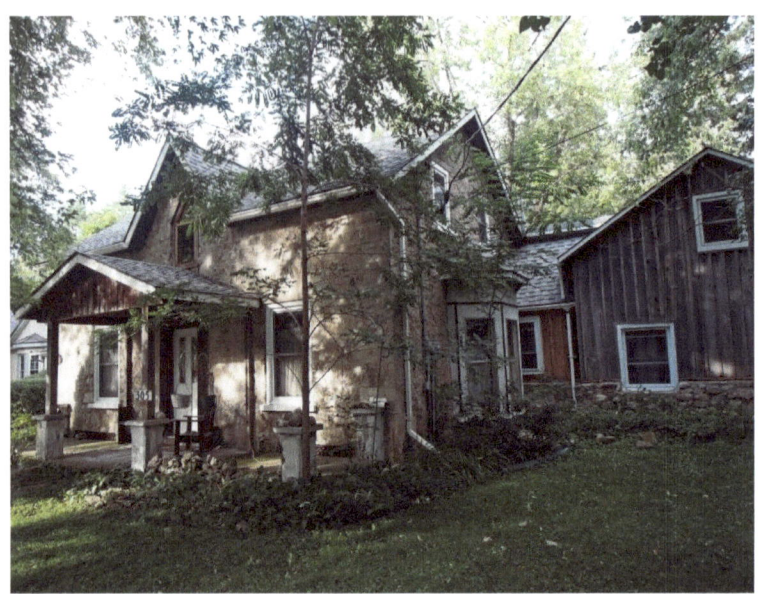

305 Geddes Street – Gothic Revival - limestone

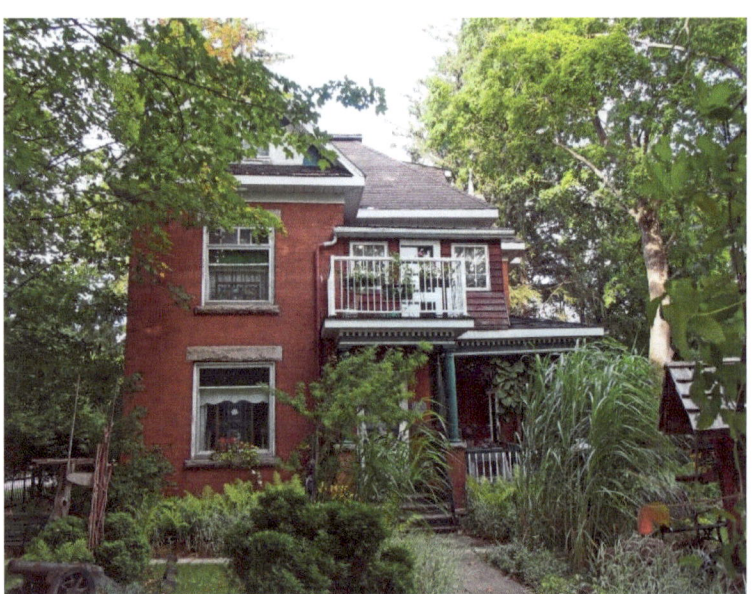

297 Geddes Street – 2½ storey tower-like bay, second floor balcony, dentil moulding above verandah with Doric columns

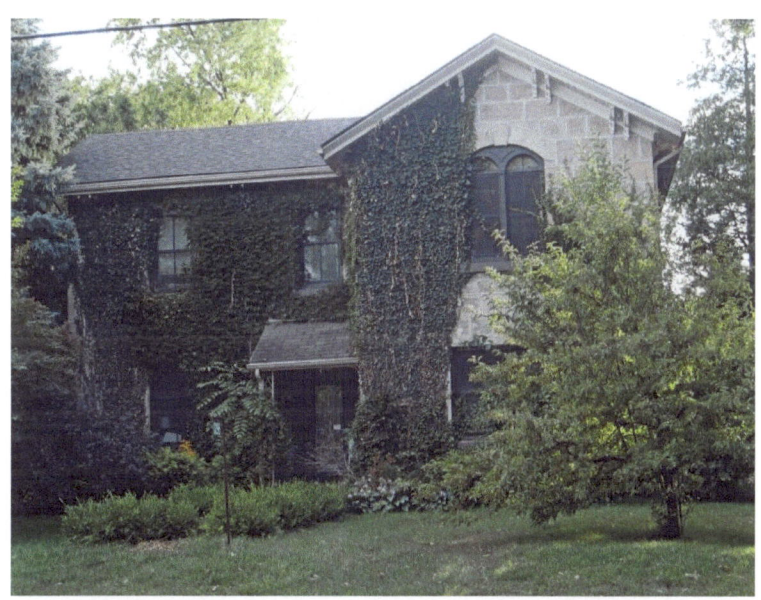

296 Geddes Street – paired cornice brackets

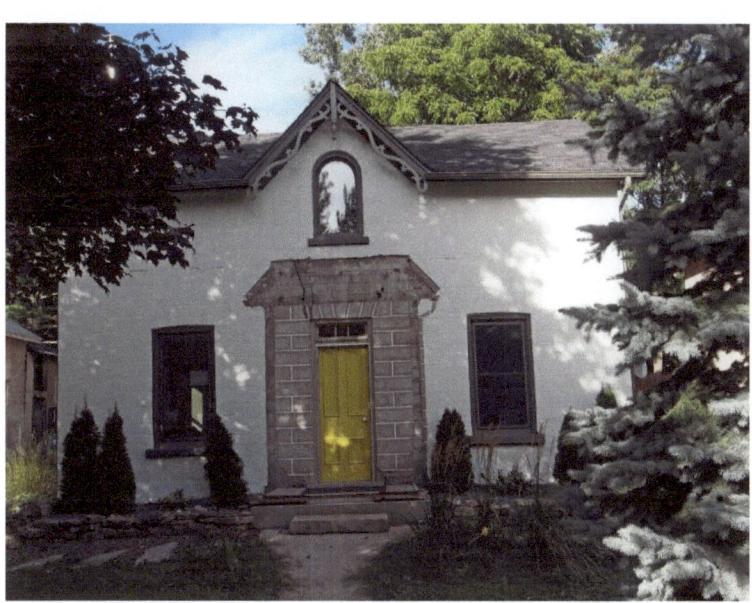

285 Geddes Street – Gothic Revival, verge board trim and finial on gable with semi-circular window and voussoirs

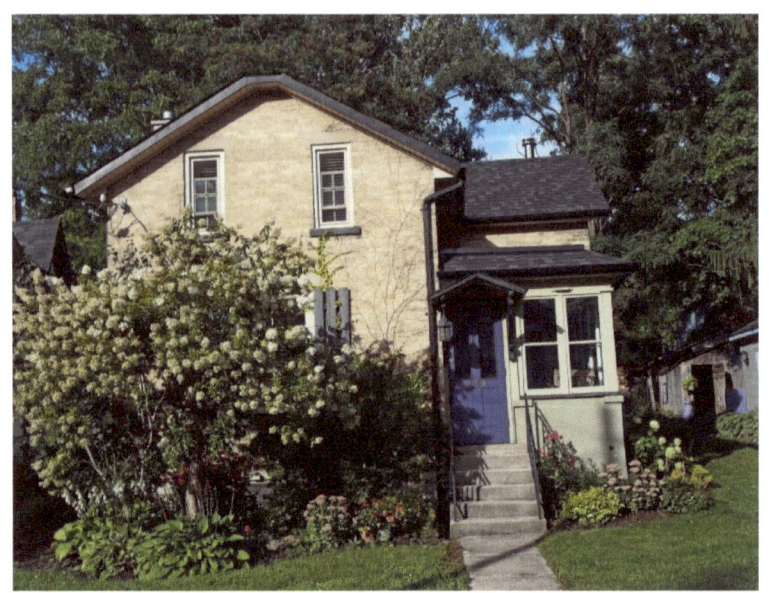

279 Geddes Street - limestone

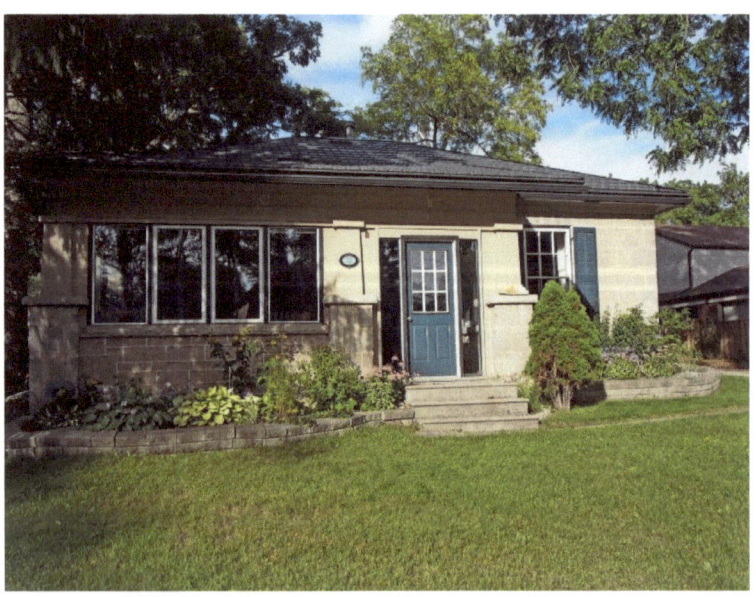

275 Geddes Street – Regency Cottage

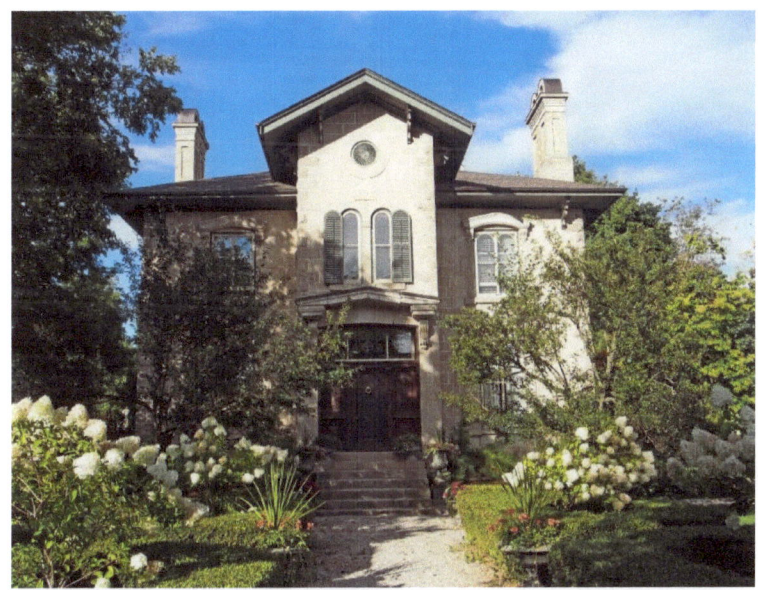

Geddes Street – c. 1854 – two-storey frontispiece, cornice brackets, window hoods, transom

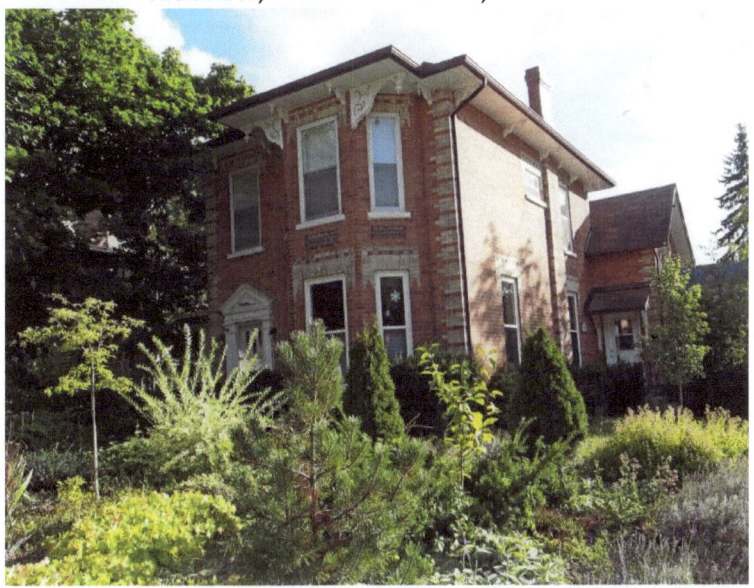

Geddes Street – Dr. John H. O'Brien, Physician – c. 1889 – Italianate, hipped roof, corner quoins, fretwork and cornice brackets, dichromatic brickwork, saw tooth moulding, entrance with engaged columns and pediment

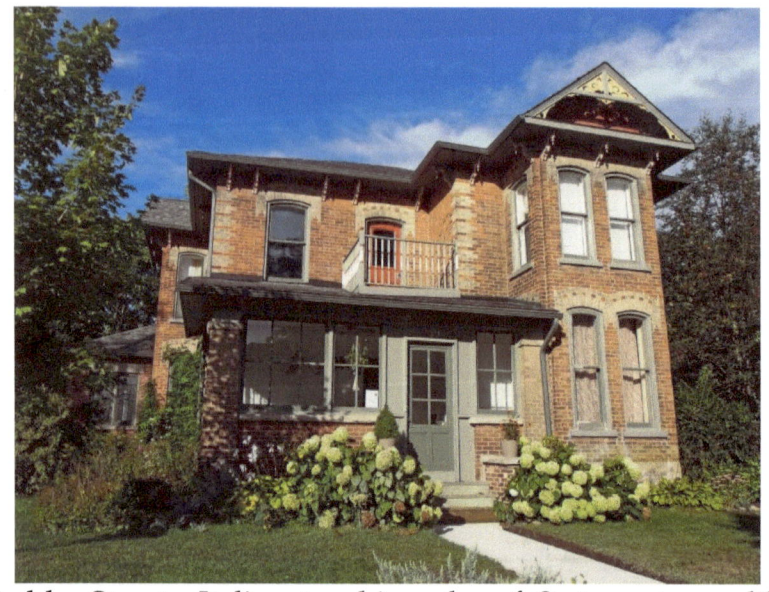

Geddes Street – Italianate – hipped roof, 2-storey tower-like bay topped with pediment with verge board trim, corner quoins, cornice brackets, voussoirs, dichromatic brickwork

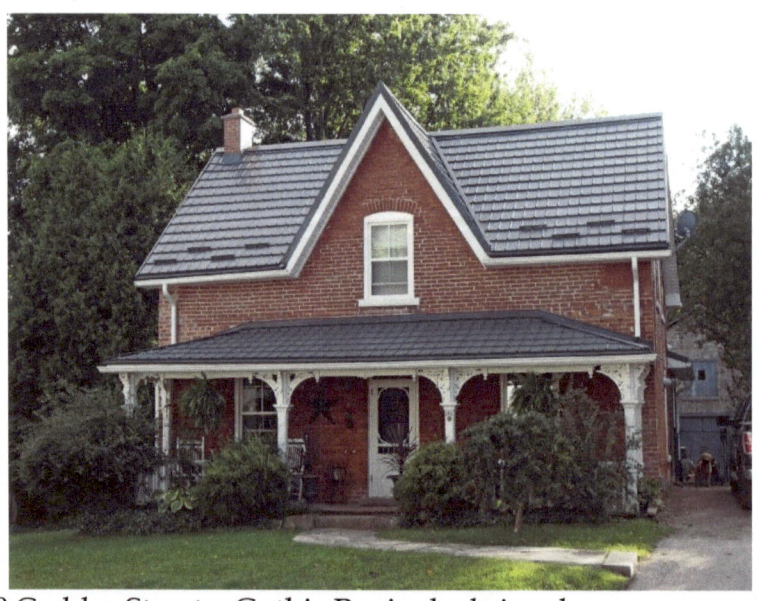

240 Geddes Street – Gothic Revival – bric-a-brac on verandah

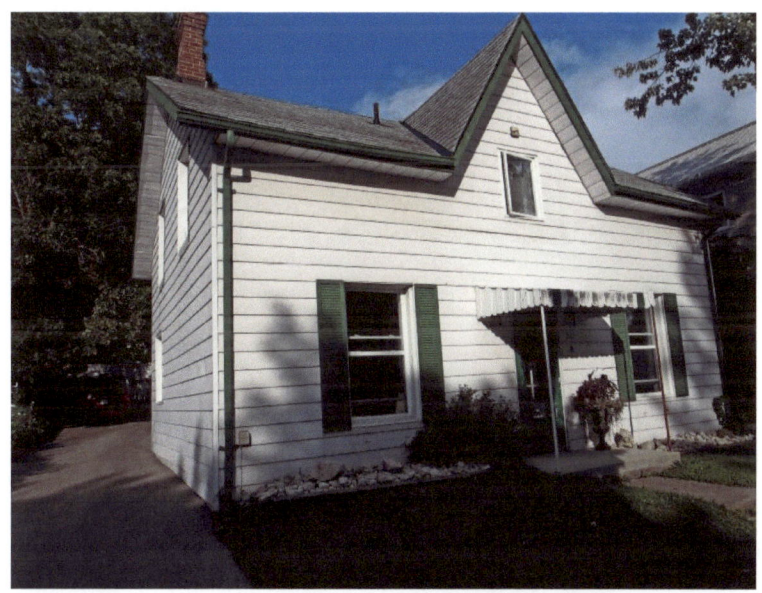

Geddes Street – Gothic Revival

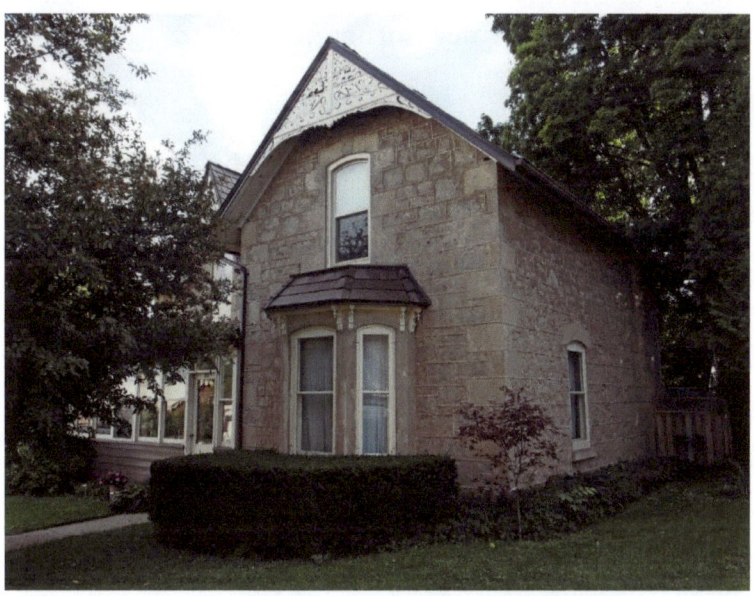

Geddes Street – Gothic Revival, verge board trim on gable,
bay window with cornice brackets

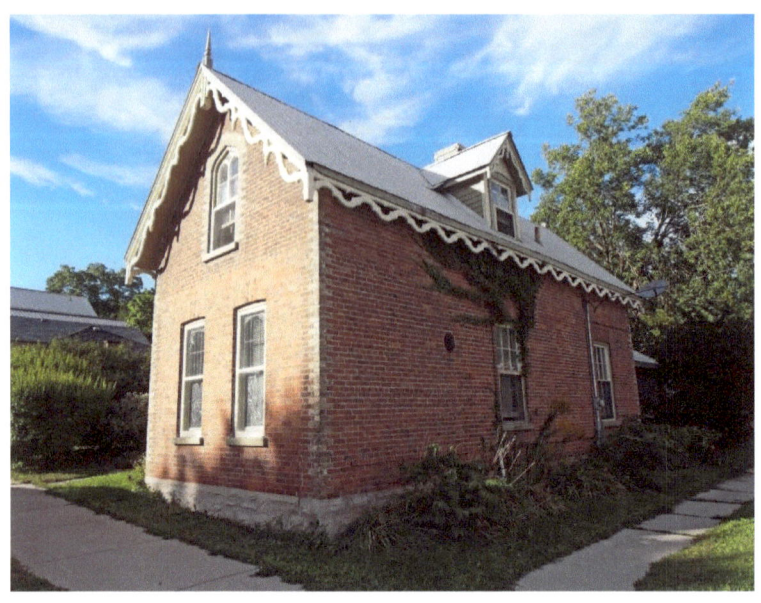

203 Geddes Street – verge board trim and finial on gable, dormer, corner quoins

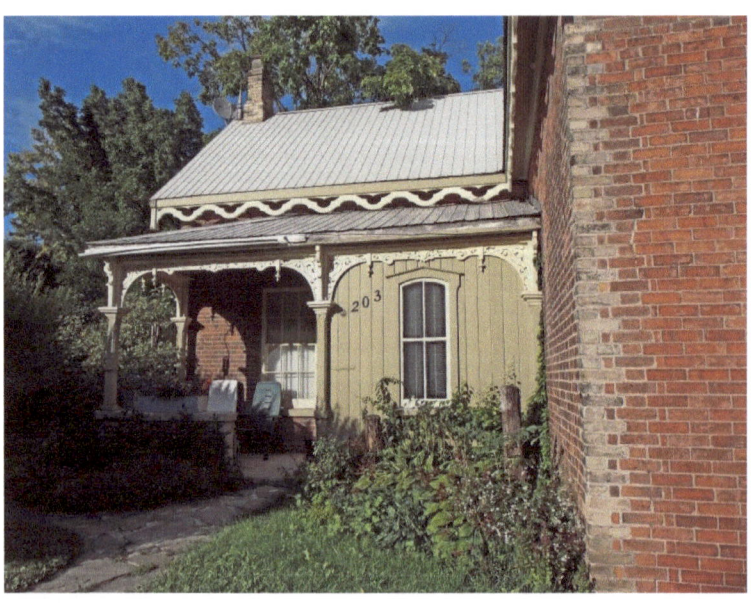

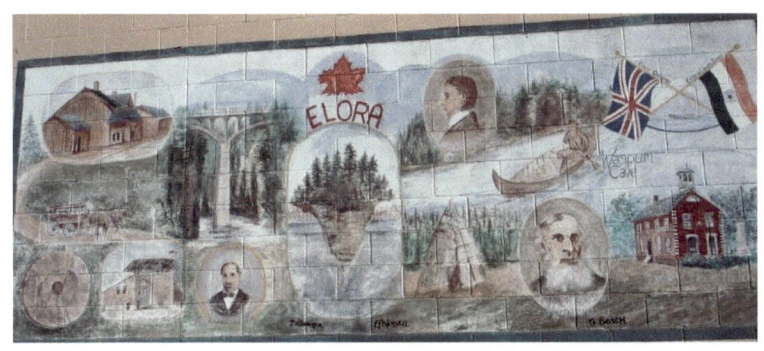

Murals

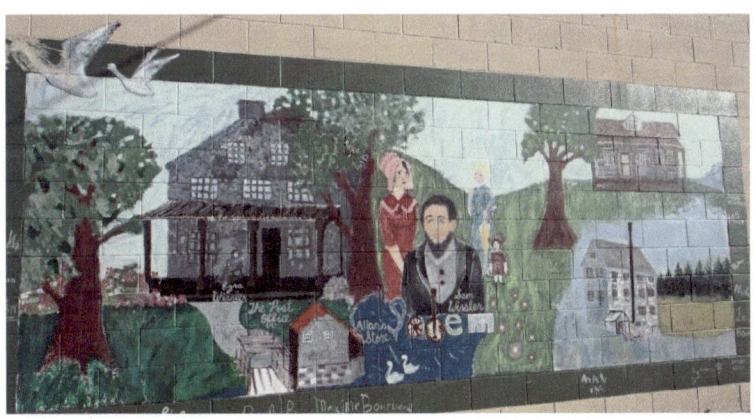

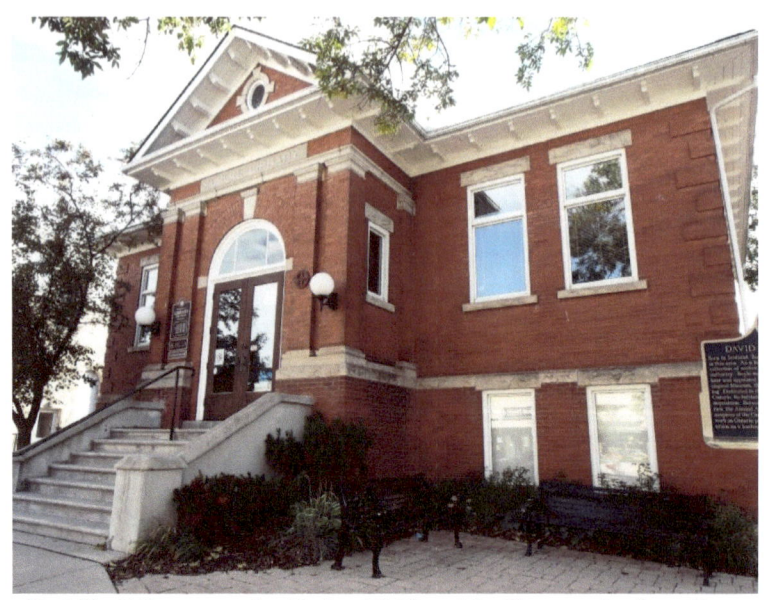

Public Library – built in 1910 with Carnegie funding

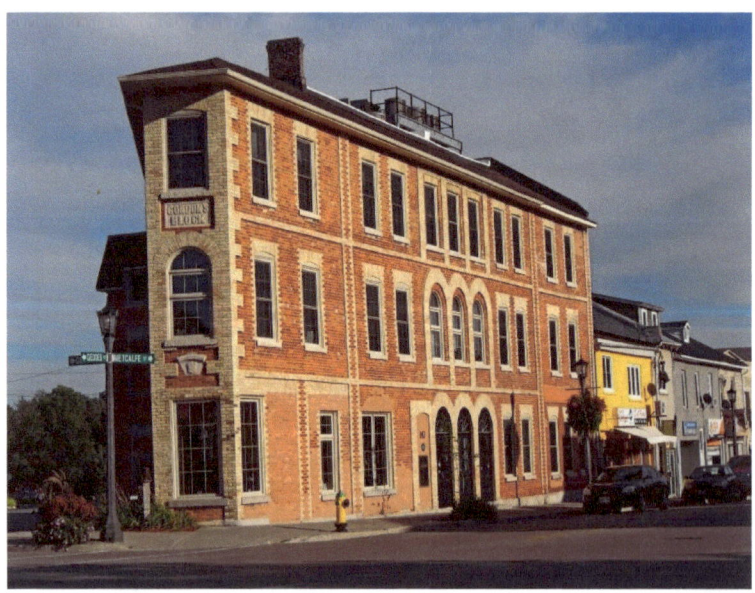

Corner of Metcalfe and Geddes Streets – Gordon's Block

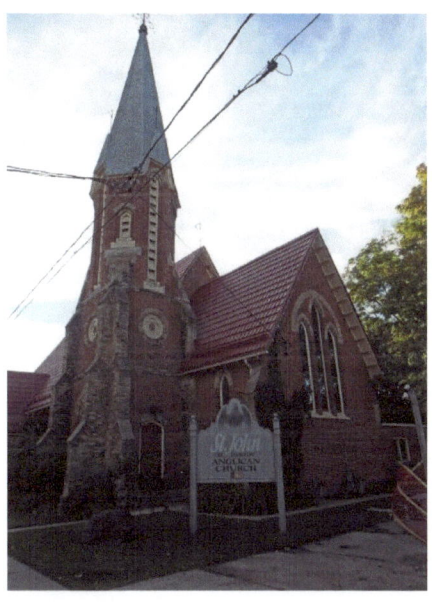

36 Henderson Street - St. John the Evangelist Anglican
Church, buttresses, dichromatic brickwork, bell tower

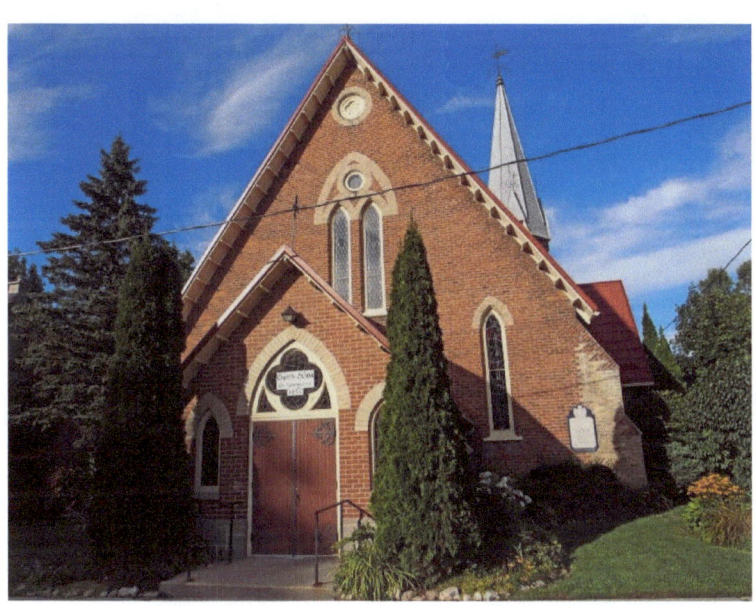

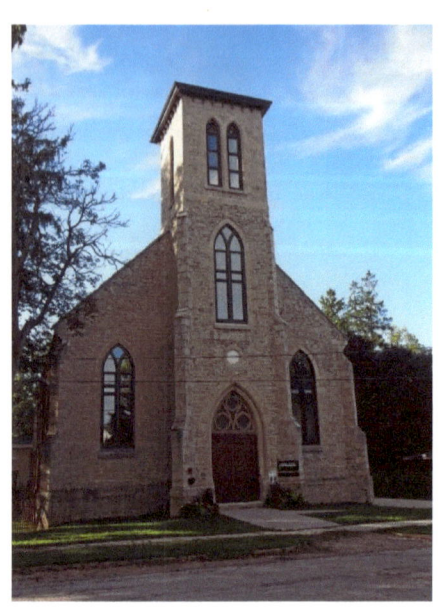

Henderson Street

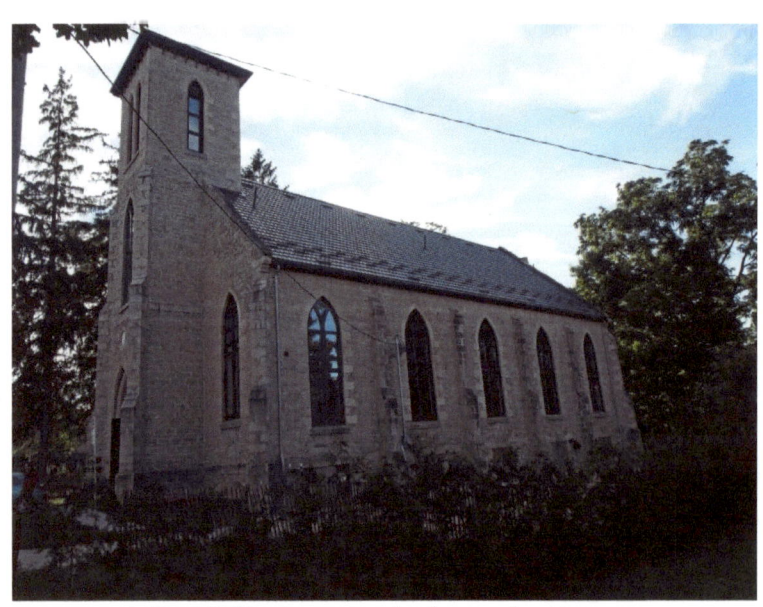

A.D. 1877 - lancet windows, buttresses

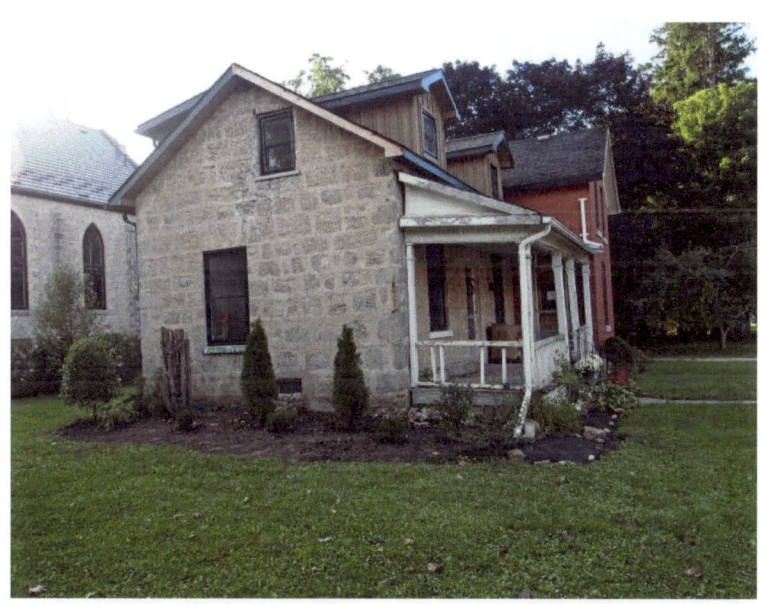

Henderson Street – limestone, dormers

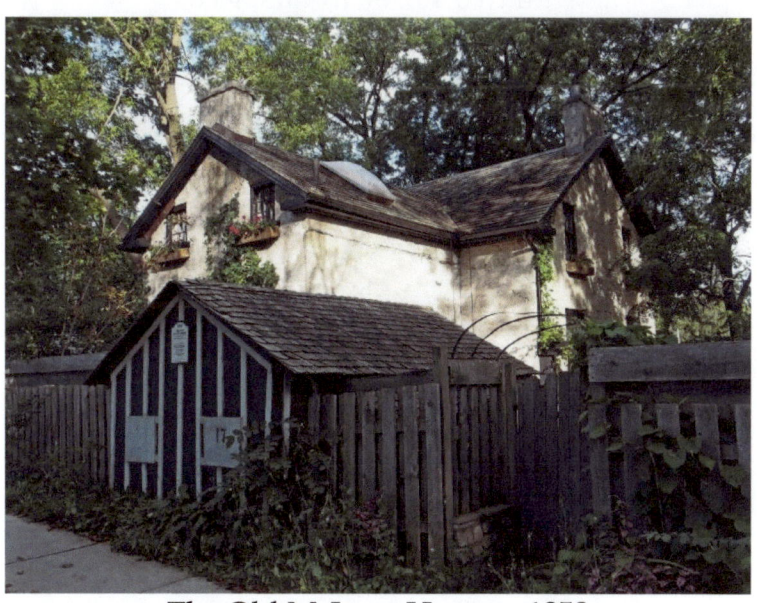

The Old McLean House – 1858

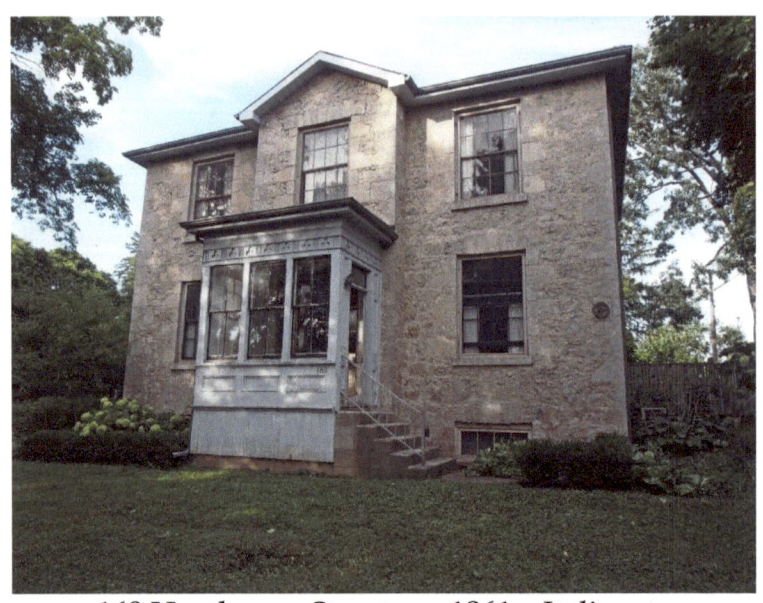

169 Henderson Street – c. 1861 – Italianate
with two-storey frontispiece

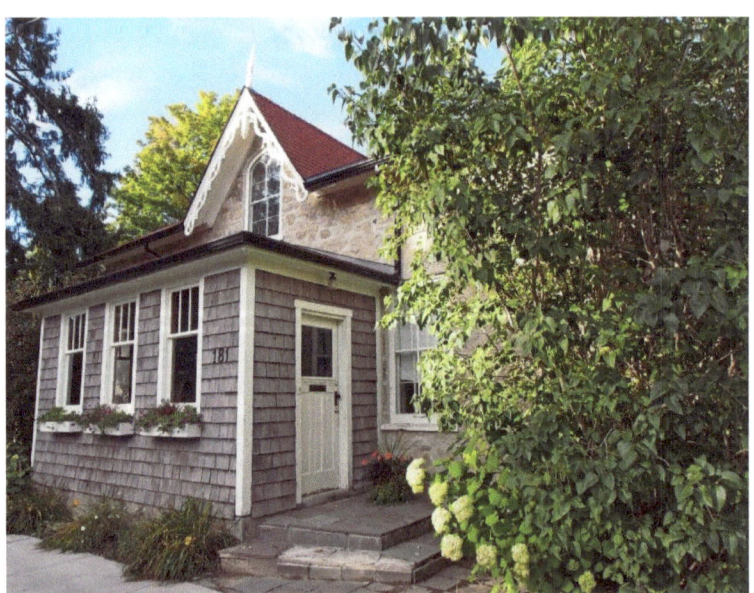

181 Henderson Street – Gothic cottage, verge board trim and
finial on gable

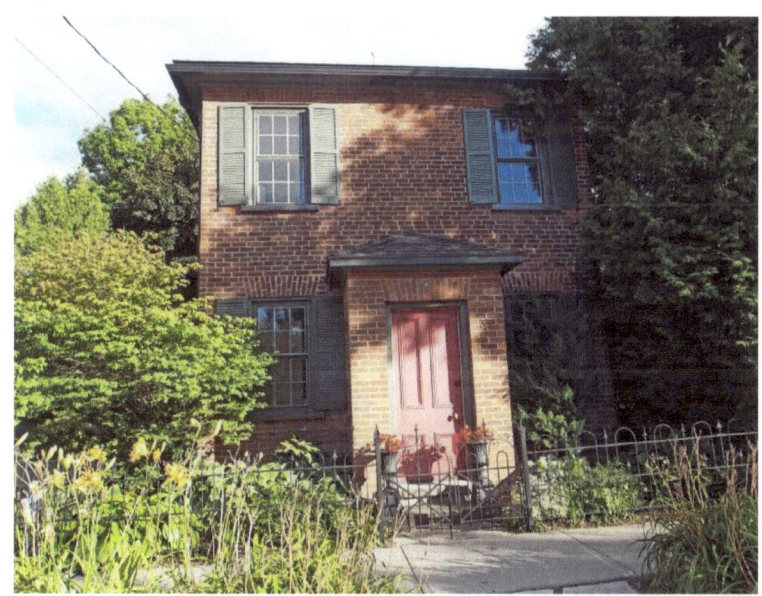

37 Henderson Street – 1832

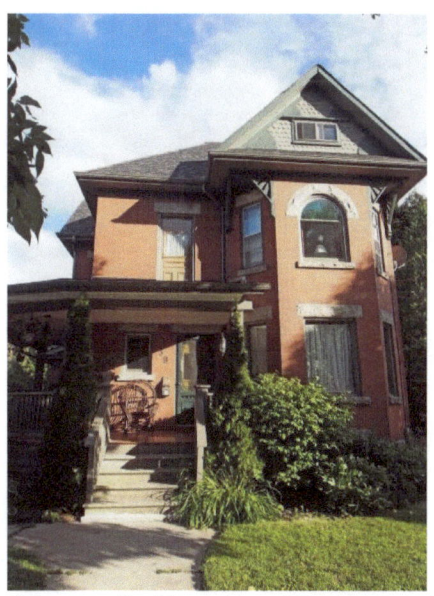

39 Henderson Street – Italianate with two-and-a-half storey
tower-like bay with fretwork, Romanesque style window arch,
wraparound verandah

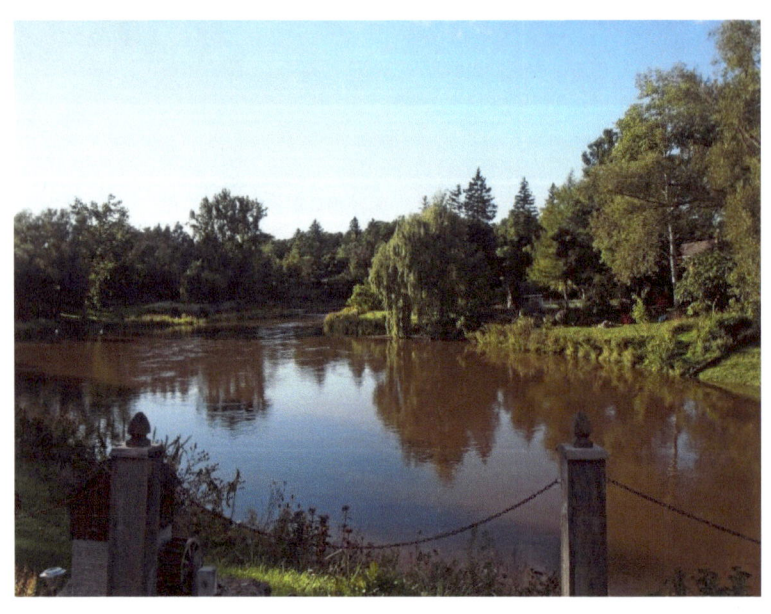

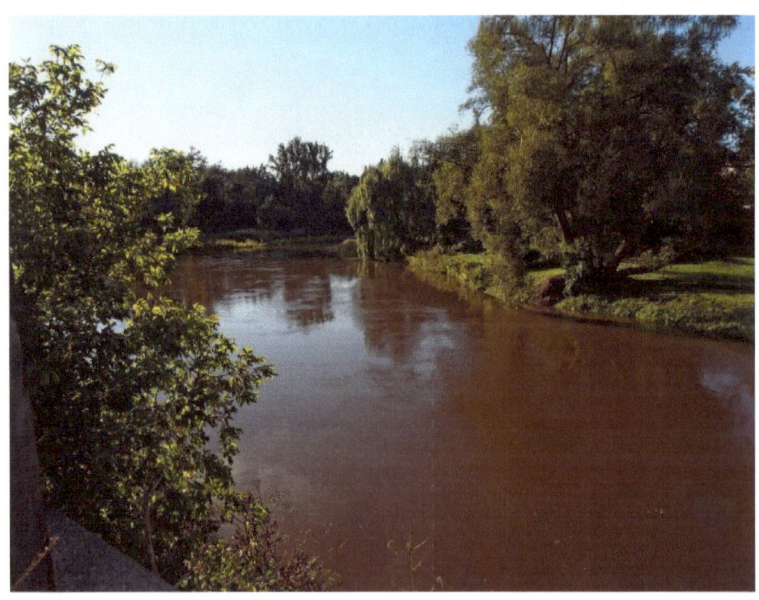

Wellington Place Museum and Archives

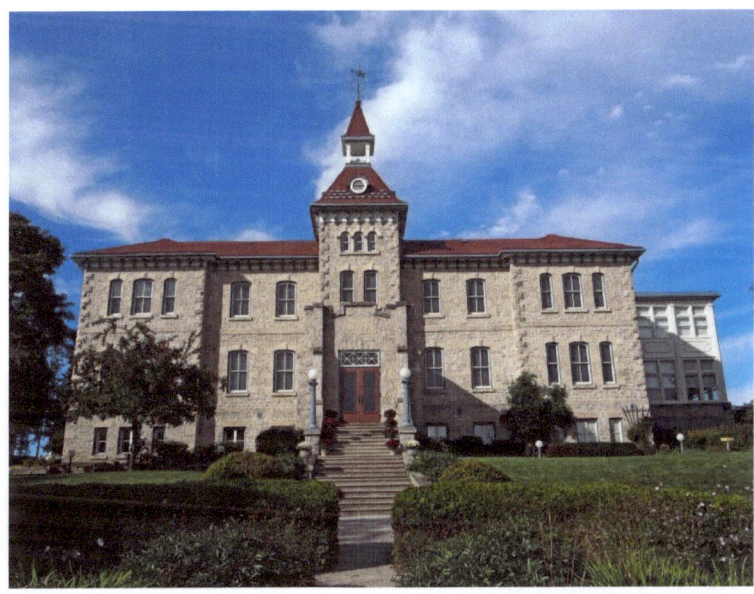

This 1877 County House of Industry and Refuge (poor house) is now a museum housing historic artifacts from the County. The museum is located in Aboyne, between Fergus and Elora. The house is in Italianate style with hipped roof, corner quoins, arched window voussoirs and keystones, cornice brackets, and a three-storey bell tower.

Architectural Terms

Brackets: a decorative or weight-bearing structural element which forms a right angle with one side against a wall and the other under a projecting surface such as an eave or roof. Example: 120 Mill Street East, Page 19	
Buttress: a masonry structure built against or projecting from a wall which serves to support or reinforce the wall. In Canadian architecture, they are sometimes used for decoration. Example: 36 Henderson Street, Page 35	
Cornice: originally the wooden overhang of the roof. With the use of stone, brick, iron and steel, the cornice is any projecting shelf at the top of a ceiling or roof. They can be very decorative. Example: Wellington County Museum, Page 41	
Cornice Return: decorative element on the end of a gable. Example: 82 Mill Street, Page 19	
Dentil Moulding: an even series of rectangles used as ornamental decoration in cornices. Example: 64 Price Street, Page 24	
Dichromatic brickwork: the use of two colours of brick, tile or slate to decorate a façade.

Example: 36 Henderson Street, Page 35 | |

Dormer: (French for "sleep") a gable end window that pierces through the plane of a sloping roof surface to create usable space in the top floor or attic of a building by adding headroom. Example: 203 Geddes Street, Page 32	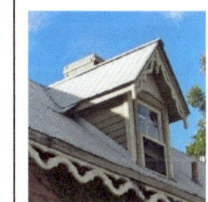
Fretwork: interlaced decorative design resembling a bracket Example: Geddes Street, Page 29	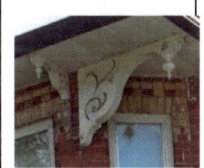
Gable: the triangular portion of a wall between the edges of a sloping roof. Example: The Misses Gilbert School for Young Ladies, Page 18	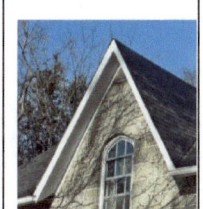
Hipped Roof: a roof where all sides slope downwards to the walls with no gables. Example: Old stone building, Page 17	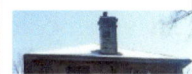
Keystones and Voussoirs: a voussoir is a wedge-shaped element used in building an arch. A keystone is the central stone that locks all the stones into position, allowing the arch to bear weight. A keystone is often enlarged and embellished. Example: Wellington County Museum, Page 41	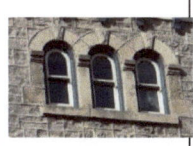

Lancet Window: a tall, narrow window with a pointed arch at its top. Example: Page 36	
Palladian Window: a large window that is divided into three sections with the centre section larger than the two side sections and usually arched. Example: Church Street, Page 23	
Pediment: a triangular section above the horizontal structure (entablature), typically supported by columns. The inside of the triangle is called the tympanum. Example: 64 Price Street, Page 24	
Quoin: masonry blocks at the corner of a wall, often a decorative feature, usually larger or of a different colour than the rest of the wall. Example: Wellington County Museum and Archives, Page 41	
Verge board and Finial: also called bargeboards – hang from the projecting end of a roof and are often elaborately carved and ornamented. **Finial:** ornament added to the top of a gable, pinnacle, canopy or spire – a Gothic element. Example: 285 Geddes Street, Page 27	

Building Styles

Gothic Revival, 1830-1890 – These decorative buildings have sharply-pitched gables with highly detailed verge boards, pointed-arch window openings, and dichromatic brickwork. It is a common style in Ontario. Example: #190, Page 17	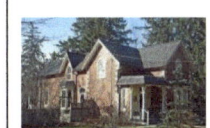
Italianate, 1850-1900 – It has wide-bracketed eaves, belvederes, wrap-around verandahs. Example: 120 Mill Street East, Page 19	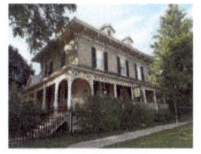